THE
PATTERSON PRINCIPLES
OF SELLING

revived and revised by

JEFFREY GITOMER

the modern leader of salesmanship
author of **The Sales Bible**

Lito Press • Charlotte, N.C.

ISBN 0-9719468-0-9

BuyGitomer, Inc. • 310 Arlington Avenue Loft 329 • Charlotte, NC 28203

www.gitomer.com • www.trainone.com • 704/333-1112 • salesman@gitomer.com

The Patterson Principles of Selling

ISBN: 0-9719468-0-9

Preview Edition II $19.95

E-mail Lito Press at Patterson@LitoPress.biz

To order additional copies of this title,
contact your local bookstore or call 704.333.1112.
The author may be contacted at the following address:
BuyGitomer
310 Arlington Avenue, Loft 329
Charlotte, NC 28203
Phone 704.333.1112, fax 704.333.1011
E-mail: salesman@gitomer.com
Web sites: www.gitomer.com, www.trainone.com

Researched and edited by Amanda Desrochers, Rachel Russotto, and Laura Miller.
Cover design by Adam Sakoonserksadee.
Page design by Greg Russell.
Cover photography by Mitchell Kearney.

THE
PATTERSON
PRINCIPLES
OF SELLING

revived and revised by

JEFFREY GITOMER

the modern leader of salesmanship
author of **The Sales Bible**

"People don't like
to be sold,
but they love to buy."

Jeffrey Gitomer, 1989

"If the prospect
understood
the proposition,
he would not have to
be sold; he would
come to buy."

John Patterson, 1889

TABLE OF CONTENTS

INTRODUCTION

"People don't like to be sold, but they love to buy," is a registered trademark phrase of mine. It's my sales mantra. I have used it for years.

My research director, Amanda Desrochers, screamed, "Jeffrey! Listen to this!" She read, "If the prospect understood the proposition, he would not have to be sold; he would come to buy. It's a Patterson quote." She chortled with delight. "You guys have the same thoughts!"

I was not surprised, but I was amazed (and gratified) at the similarity of our philosophy. And the span of time where so little has changed.

One hundred years separated those statements, but they are philosophically less than a centimeter apart.

There's an old saying that goes, "The more things change, the more they remain the same." Like many sayings, it's old because it's true.

JOHN PATTERSON
President, The National Cash Register Company

This book is your opportunity to learn selling at the feet of John Patterson, the founder and President of The National Cash Register Company, and the original master salesman of America. And keep in mind that these successful principles were created before things like the telephone or the automobile. Paved roads were not yet the order of the day. The Wright Brothers (also from Dayton) had not yet flown. Steam and coal were the predominant power. War veterans were from the Civil War. Wanna travel? Stagecoach or train. The wild west was still wild. No traffic on the freeway. No cars. Edison was cranking on the light bulb. It was the beginning of the manufacturing revolution in America. And John Patterson decided to take a leadership position.

I got the idea to revise The Patterson Principles of Selling after doing a program for NCR at their annual sales conferences in Miami and Cannes.

As a sales historian, I had always known of Patterson, but had no idea of his depth of strategies and achievements. He never wrote a commercial book on selling. "This guy is the Father of American salesmanship," I thought to myself. "And his principles are buried."

It was Patterson who created the original personality sales model. It was Patterson who created the first book on how to deal with objections. It was Patterson who held the first sales boot camps. In tents. In fields. Patterson didn't call potential customers prospects or suspects, he referred to them as "Probable Purchasers". And it was Patterson who coined the word THINK! that everyone credits to Watson and IBM. What people don't know is that Watson worked for Patterson and took it when he left, and used it to help begin the legend of IBM. Think about that.

I called NCR, told them my idea to bring Patterson's principles into the 21st century, and they said "yes" on the phone. Cool. I'll do all the research and discover his original strategies that built a multi-million dollar empire at the turn of the last century, and convert the strategies to computer and cell phone technology.

Off to Dayton, Ohio.

Amanda and I were going to a barbeque place for dinner. We arrived in Dayton to do Patterson research for the book at the historical society. The restaurant had a 20-minute wait. I decided to take a walk around the neighborhood.

Three blocks later, we came to an old building that looked like a castle split in half with a gate in the middle. "It's a graveyard," I said. "Let's go check it out." I know this sounds goofy, but it was a beautiful place.

The weather cooperated. Cloudy on the verge of a storm. Dusk. Real cemetery weather. There was a car at the gate. Security at a graveyard? Everyone's already dead. I asked the guard if we could enter. "We're about to close, you'll have to exit on the other side of the welcome center."

"No problem." I assured him. "Anyone famous buried here?" "The Wright Brothers." He bragged. "Cool," I said. "Anyone else?" "Here's a map," he offered. "Is John Patterson buried here?" I asked. "Sure is. He's in area nine at the Patterson knoll." He pointed.

I grabbed the map and searched. Found it. As we started walking, it began to drizzle. The only thing missing was a vampire. Giant trees made it light and dark at the same time. It was a huge undulating park with thousands of grave markers. Some as ornate as I've ever seen. Some 50 feet tall. We found dates back to the early 1800's.

"Over here!" I yelled as I spotted what I thought was the Patterson gravesite. A huge marble arch marked the spot for the Patterson family. About a hundred names on it. On one wall was a brief bio of John, but I couldn't find his actual stone. Every Patterson family member had the same head stone. Smaller than a ten pound sack of sugar. "Found it!" I screamed. Suddenly I went silent. I just stood on his grave imagining what he was like.

And then a flood of emotion came over me as I imagined the struggle, the risk, the creativity, the pioneering, the leadership, the setbacks, the victory, and every conceivable episode of business life when ultimate success occurs. The vision.

One hundred and eighteen years after his NCR adventure began, as I stood on the grave of John Patterson, an energy ran through my body that told me I was meant to be there. Ever get a feeling like that? Powerful and frightening at the same time.

I was inspired. I was energized. I was ready to take on this century-old task as though I was chosen for it.

Rain was falling as we left. "Pretty cool, huh?" I meekly offered to Amanda. "Unreal. What were the chances of this happening?" she said. "I wonder if it was a long shot or a predetermined one?"

Looking at the sky and the skyline I said, "Serendipity, I've been told, is God's way of remaining anonymous."

I have chosen, and I have been chosen, to share this information. To take the principles, philosophies, and sales strategies of John Patterson, and memorialize them for the twenty-first century.

When you read them you will find as I did that they are as (or more) valid today as they were then. Take them for yourself. Take them for your sales. Take them to the bank.

Jeffrey Gitomer
chief executive salesman

FATHER OF AMERICAN SALESMANSHIP?

John Patterson was a visionary. He was a thinker; he was a risk-taker; he was a reader; he was an entrepreneur; he was a teacher; he was a student; and he was a salesman. Certainly the best salesman of his time. Arguably the best salesman of all time. Patterson's success was due to his ability to blend the emotion that makes the sale with the logic that figures out the reasoning behind it. He had the perfect blend of logic and emotion. Forming opinions or justifying decisions leans toward being logical, but Patterson understood that the process of buying was an emotional one.

He knew it. ***And*** he taught it.

Not just a business man, Patterson was the creator of most of the practices which distinguish modern American business from all other businesses in the world. Not just a salesman, he was the founder of modern salesmanship. Not just a speaker, he was among the most effective of public demonstrators. Not just a financer, he was the chief exponent of getting money by spending money. Not just a manufacturer, he was the originator of the modern American factory. Not just a judge or a picker of men, he was the father of organized business and the developer of more business leaders than any other man of his time. Not just a man of commanding personality, he was a rare leader of men -- equally sure of himself in threatened defeat or in expected victory.

He is salesmanship's father because of …

The strategies he created.

The methods he pioneered.

The manner in which he transferred his genius to his team.

And their track record of success to prove it.

He is salesmanship's father because he was the first person who realized a customer was more likely to complete a transaction through buying than selling. He created the original "pull through" model. He pioneered sales training. He taught his men to adapt and harmonize with the "Probable Purchaser" (which we now erroneously call the "prospect"). He inspired his people with ideas that worked. And he backed his salespeople with advertising and promotion so that the NCR brand of cash register was by far the machine of choice.

But far and away, the overwhelming evidence of his genius was his concept of …

"Creating the demand for a receipt, rather than just trying to sell the concept of a cash register."

CONCEPTS AND STRATEGIES?

He read.

Patterson regarded a good book as a great mental possession. Only books worthy of being read again and again were to be found in his private library. All his books are marked and underlined cover to cover. Whenever new knowledge appeared, Patterson underlined it, book-marked it, studied it, **and put it into practice**.

Many underlined passages in his books show the essence of the message that captured his attention. Books helped to shape the man and the empire he built. Patterson believed that a good book was not the plaything for the idle hour, but a veritable means for generating power.

He read. *And* he generated power.

AUTHOR'S PERSONAL NOTE: *The guy before Napoleon Hill.* The person Napoleon Hill emulated was Orison Swett Marden. He was the original positive attitude genius of the 20th century. Lately I have been buying every Marden book I can get my hands on (for a list go to www.gitomer.com and enter the word MARDEN into the GitBit box).

About two years ago I purchased a bunch of books from the original John Patterson library; most of them were on longevity, and a few biographies. I was perusing the books last week to complete this work and decided to look at every book that I owned of Patterson's. I pulled out the title, "He Can Who Thinks He Can" by Orison Swett Marden. My blood ran cold. It is a first edition book published in 1908 and I realized yet one more thing in common. Smiled. And went about my business.

I carry the Marden book from Patterson's library with me now, and read a page or two a day.

I especially read the parts that Patterson underlined. As usual, he found the gems. Here are a few:

QUOTES UNDERLINED BY THE HAND OF JOHN PATTERSON TAKEN FROM THE BOOK

"HE CAN WHO THINKS HE CAN"

BY ORISON SWETT MARDEN
PUBLISHED IN 1908

Every child should be taught to expect success.

People do not realize the immense value
of utilizing spare minutes.

Multitudes of people, enslaved by bad physical habits,
are unable to get their best selves into their work.

Some of the greatest men in history never discovered
themselves until they lost everything but their pluck and grit.

Almost anybody can resolve to do a great thing;
it is only the strong, determined character that puts
the resolve into execution.

No substitute has ever yet been discovered for honesty.

Happiness is a condition of mind.

Resolve that you will be a man of ideas,
always on the lookout for improvement.

Power gravitates to the man who knows how and why.

There is no word in the English language
more misused and abused than luck.

EVOLUTION AND POWER OF THE RECEIPT

Never forget the genius associated with the philosophy: **Patterson did not sell the register, rather he created the need and the demand for a receipt.** This may be the most powerful business strategy of the 19th and 20th century. Take a minute to ponder how you might use that philosophy to build your business. What demands are you creating? Who is calling you to buy?

Add to this incredible reality that the receipt is one of the most powerful pieces of paper in the world. Every receipt has its own power. It's your PROOF of purchase and ownership. And EVERY purchase is now accompanied by one. Thanks to John Patterson.

Receipts not only prove you bought it. They prove you own it, can return it, can exchange it, can get a warranty enforced, can resell it, can get reimbursed for it, can deduct it from your taxes, and much, much more. In many cases you need to show your receipt to exit a store thirty seconds after you just made the purchase.

You save receipts for years. They often outlive the very product you bought.

Think of how often you use your receipts ... they are documents, they are the reminders marking the passage of your time and your money. Receipts are the one constant in business for the last 100 years. *Would you like your receipt in the bag?*

The receipt is the only thing in business that has remained intact. A receipt is the "Prize" because without it, you have lost.

Banking and checking accounts give receipts for transactions. Your cancelled check or credit card statement is your receipt. A receipt is not just a proof of purchase -- it's a recorded transaction. Proof of payment, with clerk, date, time, etc. It's a valuable document of who did what, when they did it, and how much was involved.

Want your money back? Better have your receipt.
IRS knocking at your door? Better have your receipts.

*"**Do you want a receipt with that?**"* came way before
*"**Do you want fries with that?**"*

NCR promotional photo used in the early 1900s.

"A receipt, like a deed, is proof of title
to property."   — *1912 quote from a*
National Cash Register brochure

"Try to get a refund without one."
                          — *Jeffrey Gitomer*

THE EVOLUTION
OF THE PRIMER
THE FIRST SALES TRAINING MANUAL.

John Patterson did not just believe in the power of training, he lived the essence of it. Early on he realized that training was the link to infinite sales.

The first NCR sales script, "How I Sell A National Cash Register," which became known as *The Primer*, contained instructions on what salesmen should say during a sale, and what they were to do while saying it. The Primer covered the factors which were common to every sale.

It divided the sale into 4 parts:
1. The approach to the prospect
2. The demonstration of the register
3. How to overcome objections
4. How to close the sale

This sequence of ideas become the steps to a sale. The first Primer was introduced in June of 1887 at the agent's convention.

It left out a few steps, but hey -- not bad for 120 years old.

The Primer began when Joe Crane, Patterson's brother-in-law, and their best salesman, was asked to sit in on a meeting devoted to the discussion of prices. At the end of the meeting, Crane stated that the price was alright and the product was good, but they didn't know how to sell it. **Crane saw that the salesmen were selling in the purchaser's environment.** That is where the problem started. Here they were more susceptible to distractions. Sales distractions. It was much better to take the purchaser elsewhere.

This idea worked phenomenally for Crane, and Patterson wanted his salesmen to follow Crane's lead. Crane said the same thing, word for word, during each demonstration to his probable purchasers.

At first, Patterson thought this would become monotonous and tiresome, but Crane replied, "It has never got monotonous yet. The reason it is not monotonous is because it is to different people every time." Crane presented Patterson with one of his demonstrations, after which Patterson stated, "I will call the stenographer; you dictate this to him and get it typewritten."

1887

1923

"We progress through change."

— *Patterson's favorite quote*

Patterson made copies and sent them to all of his sales agents (12 at that time) with a note: "Crane sells more machines than any of you fellows, and he sells them this way. I suggest that you all learn this." He published it and called it "How I Sell A National Cash Register" by J.H. Crane. (In those days, men used their initials rather than their full name. Even in signing.)

After reading the script, Patterson's men felt there was "too much Crane in it" so he revised the text and published it as the NCR Primer.

The Primer was the first documented sales training tool.

Patterson felt the use of a standardized presentation would make a good salesman a better one. His men had to memorize this Primer word for word. Patterson's thinking was if his men knew The Primer word for word, and said it so many times, they would never forget what they said during any demonstration.

Was it the best system in the world? -- No, but it WORKED. And it worked well in those times. Even though you don't want to sound mechanical, there's something to be said for repeating a formula that works.

Patterson tested his men's ability to repeat the text on a continuous basis. If someone replied in a 'schoolboy' fashion or did not recite it naturally or spontaneously, he would send them off to Dayton for a course of training. When the salesman had committed The Primer to memory, no interruptions could throw him off track.

The reputation of Patterson is not a benevolent one. He was strict, and all business at all times. And, let's face it, there weren't many distractions in those days. No TV, no computers, no cars, and no shopping malls. Newspapers, magazines, the mail, and rumors were the primary method of information transfer.

Concentration on a single purpose was easier to say the least, and Patterson had an obsession for this.

As The Primer grew, so did the selling strategies and concepts. The Primer addressed everything from dressing to closing. And it detailed the first personality and situational selling methodology. It became their bible of selling (not to be confused with The Sales Bible that appeared 100 years later).

By 1923 The Primer was mature. It had expanded into two volumes: A "Manual" and "Selling Helps."

Manual for N.C.R. Salesmen 1923 Edition

This manual contains selling methods used by the most successful sales representatives. It's divided into 5 parts …

> **NCR Salesmanship:** An NCR salesman is made up of 5 components: health, honesty, knowledge, courage, and hard work.

> **Suggestions for Study:** Three areas to focus on are the need for the resister, the salesman's actual knowledge of the register, and the selling process.

> **Store Systems and Their Weak Points:** Patterson wanted each of his salesman to be familiar with the various store systems in use and the weak points of each. Knowing the weak points strengthened the sale.

> **The Value of National Cash Register Functions:** The greatest VALUE a register delivers is the PRINTED RECEIPT, along with a detailed strip, automatic and multiple cash drawers.

> **The Selling Plan:** This section discussed the 5 steps to make a sale:
> > **1.** Interesting the merchant
> > **2.** Explaining the register
> > **3.** Closing the sale
> > **4.** Installing the register
> > **5.** Serving the merchant

The Manual ends with a lesson on the value and importance of keeping physically fit, and a chart detailing the 50 Ways I Can Improve Myself …

50 ways
I can improve myself

Physically

① Simple food, quality, quantity.
② Regularity in eating and sleep.
③ Masticate; leave table hungry.
④ We are a part of all we have eaten.
⑤ Exercise, five minutes, three times daily.
⑥ Air—most important.
⑦ Sunlight, artificial light.
⑧ Water inside and outside.
⑨ Loose clothing.
⑩ Early to sleep; get plenty.

Mentally

① Think sanely.
② Learn from mental superiors.
③ Learn to listen attentively.
④ Read best newspapers and books.
⑤ Improve the memory.
⑥ Concentrate.
⑦ Don't worry unnecessarily.
⑧ Be systematic.
⑨ Weigh both sides
⑩ Avoid inferior minds.

Morally

① Right is right, wrong is wrong.
② Be truthful.
③ Ignore precedent if wrong.
④ Seek elevating recreation.
⑤ Don't deceive yourself.
⑥ Learn to say "no."
⑦ Live up to your principles.
⑧ Avoid temptation.
⑨ Form good habits.
⑩ Have a constitution.

Financially

① Increase my earnings.
② Decrease unnecessary expense.
③ Save money, U. S. Postal Bank.
④ Money makes money.
⑤ Invest— don't gamble.
⑥ Make family budget.
⑦ Hard work.
⑧ Study the business.
⑨ Pay cash for everything.
⑩ Increase credit balance.

Socially

BAD ASSOCIATES

① Avoid bad associates.
② Select helpful friends.
③ Think alone.
④ Learn to be happy alone.
⑤ Family best company.
⑥ Work out, alone, my problems.
⑦ Avoid so-called society.
⑧ Entertain economically.
⑨ Stand well with neighbors.
⑩ Do some welfare work.

SELLING HELPS FOR N.C.R. SALESMEN
1923 EDITION

Patterson believed the real reason a merchant doesn't buy is because he does not know the benefits a cash register will bring to his business. Because of this, the merchant raised objections and asked questions. The Primer creates dialogue examples of the most frequently asked questions and objections, along with answers to these that have been successful to the members in the selling force. The topics covered in this manual are as old as they are modern:

Price:
"Your price is too high"

Excuses for Delay:
"I want to think about it"

Temptation:
"My clerks are all honest, they would never steal"

Interested in a Small Register:
"A single drawer register is all I need"

Receipt:
"The clerk will not give out the receipt"

Allowance (trade in) **Too Small:**
"Your allowance for my old register is not high enough"

Charge Business:
"70% of my business is charge. I am not interested in your cash register"

I am Satisfied with my Present System:
"Our present system is fast enough"

One hundred years later, the SAME excuses still pervade the selling process.

Also included in "Selling Helps" are experiences and stories from NCR salesmen, how to approach a prospect, a history of the cash register, its ten stages of development, and an article written by Patterson about why he truly felt the need for a receipt. This book captures the essence of what to do in the real-world from people who are doing it every day.

Each volume of The Primer was numbered and assigned to a salesman. If he quit or was terminated, he had to turn it in. That statement alone shows you what power and respect they gave the document.

When I first read The Primer in the Montgomery County Historical Society where the Patterson archives are preserved, it was like I was reading the Holy Grail or the Talmud.

Ancient sales philosophies, methods and strategies, that were still valid today.

The pages that follow are The Patterson Principles of Selling. They have been extracted from The Primer, and other writings by and about Patterson.

I have taken the liberty to change a few words as they apply to sales 100 years later.

What is a principle you ask?

A principle is a concept. A strategy. A thought that when understood, practiced, and implemented into your sales process, becomes part of your philosophy, rather than simply a technique. Principles are the highest form of action and self belief. "Give me liberty or give me death!" is a principle.

I have uncovered 34 major sales principles of John Patterson.

I believe they capture the essence of what he preached and practiced. I have also added my 21st century adaptations and concepts to implement these strategies into your selling quest for success. Many of them spill over from sales to life. All the better. All the more powerful.

I have taken the liberty to adjust a word here and there without violating the Patterson way of thinking ... our philosophies are so similar it's scary. And I have added one of my own. It's the .5 in the 34.5 Principles. It's the one that glues the others together. But the real question you're asking right now is:

"Hey Gitomer, what's in this for me?"

Here's what you will find for you as you read each principle …

THE PATTERSON PRINCIPLE

THE QUOTES (one from John, one from me -- and an occasional one from someone else relevant). The quotes emphasize the principle.

THE DESCRIPTION AND EXPLANATION OF THE PRINCIPLE

THINK!
The real world application process to make you THINK -- The word THINK! will challenge you to do just that. There will be "thinks" to think about. Questions to ask yourself. You will find a THINK icon after each principle to help you understand how to think about the concept, and adapt it for yourself.

PP: **The real world application process to help you understand the mind of the Probable Purchaser** -- PP will tell you what you can do with the principle. How you can act on it. How it will help you make a sale.

THE PROBABLE PURCHASER

Patterson's selling philosophy was centered around the concept of referring to a prospect as a *Probable Purchaser* -- thus defining the prospect and your attitude towards him or her in the SAME breath! So powerful. It's the biggest sales aha I've had since I earned my first commission back in 1963 (yeah 1963). To me, PP is as powerful a sales philosophy as I have EVER seen or read -- and it's well over a hundred years old -- **AND NO ONE USES IT.**

Patterson could have used words like *prospect, possible, prospective,* and *potential,* but in his positive attitude thought process he not only assumed the sale, he put word-thoughts into the minds of his sales people so they would constantly reinforce their own belief system. *Probable Purchaser* is a classic lost element of the Patterson Principles of Selling that will not only be resurrected here, but that you can employ everyday as you seek success.

AND OF COURSE, IN THE TRUE PATTERSON FASHION, THERE WILL BE AN EXERCISE.

EXERCISE: Something you can do right now to begin mastering the principle. Convert the ideas presented into personal achievement for you. In other words, turning thoughts into actions.

These principles by themselves will not give you a sale today. They will enhance your selling process, and give you sales forever.

HERE ARE THE 34.5 PATTERSON PRINCIPLES OF SELLING ...

1. Think!

"Think and act — two words of progress."
— *John H. Patterson*

"Thinking. An action that very few people take the time to do."
— *Jeffrey Gitomer*

The word **THINK!** will carry you through the rest of the book. An action that very few people take the time to do. And a lifetime opportunity to stay ahead and succeed. Patterson believed that progress was the result of thought. The phrase **Think!** was used as a motivational tool for Patterson's salesmen as well as the rest of the workers within the company.

Thinking, like any other action, is a discipline. You decide your own outcome based on your desire and self determination. Realize early on in this writing that every principle takes action on your part to master it. And that "thought" will be the backbone of your ideas and their implementation -- your actions to succeed.

Twelve things to Think! about every day:
How can I uncover new customers?
How can I become a better presenter?
How does my customer profit from using my product?
How did I better myself today?
What did I learn new?
How can I serve better?
Is my attitude better today than it was yesterday?
Are my customers loyal today?
How am I investing my time today?
Did I get a referral today?
Did I give a referral today?
Did I work on my legacy today?
THINK about taking action on each of the twelve thoughts.

PP Most people have no idea how to spend time in thought. Try writing your thoughts as you come up with them.

AUTHORS NOTE: I have been writing my thoughts for eleven years. It's not just thinking -- it's capturing your thoughts and turning them into reality.

What have you been thinking about?

How have you turned those thoughts into actions?

Exercise: Set aside THINK! time -- make a THINK appointment every day, even if it's only 15 minutes. Decide in advance what you want to think about, and what solutions you're looking for. I know, it sounds hokey -- **but here's the gold:**

Write ideas no matter how far fetched they sound -- just write for ten minutes straight. Your stream-of-conscious thinking will net you some amazing results.

Do it for a week. The results will be so amazing, you'll do it for a lifetime.

2. Self Belief ...

The Most Convincing Characteristic of a Salesperson

"If the salesman himself has faith in the honesty of his goods, he will have little trouble in convincing his customers."

— *Frank Farrington*
(This quote was taken from an underlined book in Patterson's library.)

"Self belief is a most convincing characteristic to others, and THE most convincing characteristic to yourself."

— *Jeffrey Gitomer*

"Believe in yourself and your product."

— *1921 Manual for NCR Salesmen*

Self belief is the most convincing sales characteristic that must be mastered. You must believe you are the best salesman in the world, and you must believe you work for the best company in the world. And you must believe you are selling the best product in the world.

If you don't believe, no one else will either.

Before you can sell anyone else, you must be sold on yourself, you must be sold on your company; and you must be sold on your product.

What do you believe in?

How can you strengthen your self belief?

Do you realize that self belief is tied to your degree of success?

In order for a sale to take place, three things must be present. One -- you gotta believe that you work for the greatest company in the world. Two -- you gotta believe that you have the greatest product in world. And three -- you gotta believe that you are the greatest person in the world.

The key words are: **"You Gotta Believe."**

Strong belief will make you a more innovative, creative salesperson with a burning drive and desire to help the other person buy -- and that's a big difference from a burning drive and desire to sell something. *People don't like to be sold, but they love to buy.*

Exercise: Want an instant lesson? Go out and buy a copy of "The Little Engine That Could." Or go to your kids room and get the copy full of crayon marks. Read it regularly. **It's not just a book for kids, it's a philosophy for a lifetime.**

3. Positive Mental Attitude is Determined by You, Not Others.

"Success in selling is up to the attitude within each one of us individually."

— *John H. Patterson*

"The way you dedicate yourself to the way you think is the definition of attitude, either positive or negative. The only difference is the choice you make about the way you think."

— *Jeffrey Gitomer*

Your mental attitude is your motivation.

Positive mental attitude is the motivation and inspiration that feeds off of your self belief. Success in sales and success in service starts with a positive attitude.

Attitude is defined as the way you dedicate yourself to the way you think. Think negative or think positive is a choice and a process. **Negative** is (unfortunately) an instinctive process. **Positive** is a learned self-discipline that must be studied and practiced every day.

When you're giving any form of communication or presentation, your attitude will shine through.

Sometimes your personal sun is not shining. Things may be wrong with your family, finances, or your health.

If you let this transcend into your sales presentation and your customer communications, the consequence is low or no sales.

The result will be that you blame others for your own inability to separate your attitude from your events.

You become what you think about all day long.

— *Earl Nightingale*

Want to start making an attitude change? Take attitude actions. To achieve a POSITIVE attitude, you must take physical, verbal, and mental ACTIONS. Every day. Read two pages from a positive book at the start of every day. For a listing of positive reading books go to **www.gitomer.com**.

Exercise: The EYE Can. Cut out eyes from a magazine and glue them to a tin can. If you think you can't, look at the eye (I) can and know that you can succeed.

4. Boot Camp Separates the Salesman from the Wanna-be Salesman.

"Industry is cheap. It is laziness that costs. It has cost many a bright man a bright career."

— *John H. Patterson*

"Sales is survival, the best prepared are most likely to survive."

— *Jeffrey Gitomer*

Survival tactics, while they may not always be employed, must be mastered so that they are able to be implemented whenever the situation arises. This is not simply how to find water in the desert; this is how to beat the competition. How to sell when times are tough or how to win in any struggle or any environment. Survival is not about saving your hide; survival is about mastering a circumstance or environment and emerging victorious.

Basic training includes physical, mental, and psychological self-discipline. Intense basic training is a requirement for success in any sport, particularly the sport of selling. Patterson put his men through his own personal boot camp in order to ensure he was hiring only the BEST men for his team.

He didn't view the hiring process as hiring a salesman. Rather, he hired men who he planned to train in sales.

How much ENERGY are you putting
into your basic training?

How DEDICATED are you to
getting better at selling?

What is your personal boot camp? How would you describe it?
How do you discipline yourself on an ongoing basis? What is your
daily agenda? Consider this: What would Patterson add to YOUR
daily agenda? How well would you do in his boot camp? Would
you have survived the tasks at hand?

Exercise: Train mentally for 30 minutes a day. Give yourself that
gift for a lifetime.

Tents at Sugar Camp training site c1924.

"Boot camp is a fight for the fit.
Rigorous training is the lifeblood for
future sales (and business) success."

— *John H. Patterson*

"You can't teach an old dog new tricks.
OK, so don't train old dogs. Same with
salespeople."   — *Jeffrey Gitomer*

5. Survival is a Combination of Knowing and Doing.

"If there ever comes a time in this business when courage will not be necessary, when it will not be necessary for us to fight against obstacles, I shall know that it is time to put up the shutters, turn off the power and draw the fires for all times."

— John H. Patterson

"All salespeople know what to do. Problem is they don't do it."

— Jeffrey Gitomer

"The biggest reason people don't succeed is that they don't expose themselves to existing information." says Jim Rohn. And I add to that -- "Therefore, they don't believe in themselves enough (lack the confidence) to succeed."

It's not so important that you **want** to succeed -- it's critical you know **why** you want to succeed -- and what has **prevented** you from achieving your success to date? What **belief system and game plan** do you need to put in place to gain that success?

It's easy to lose self belief, if the one you've got in place is weak due to poor knowledge and lack of determination.

It's easy to fail at sales if you have never told yourself (sold yourself) the real reason you want sales success in the first place. Not earning money for money's sake -- *but the real reason you want the money, and what you'll do with it once you get it.*

How do you continue to educate yourself?

Are you at home filling your brain with useless television re-runs? Or are you making the most of your time and STUDYING to make yourself a better person, a better SALESperson? What have you done in the last day, week, or month to expand your knowledge?

How much time do you dedicate to your own personal achievement? Answer: Not enough. Here's a few painful questions to ponder.

1. How many books have you read on salesmanship in the last year?

2. How many books have you read on positive attitude in the last year?

3. How many books have you read on creativity in the last year?

4. How many hours did you waste watching television last week?

5. Do you get paid for watching TV? Why are you watching?

6. Could you convert or invest some of your "TV hours" into reading hours?

7. How many sales or personal development tapes do you listen to in your car?

8. How many hours of radio drivel do you listen to in the car?

9. How many hours could you convert or invest from drivel to knowledge?

10. What would that conversion be worth?

10.5 What price are you paying for not converting?

Survival is a combination of knowing and doing. What do you **KNOW**? What are you **DOING**?

 Knowing Exercise: Why do you want to succeed? Answer the question and each time you answer it, add the question "why?" again -- after four of five levels, you'll have the real why.

 Doing Exercise: What is preventing you from doing what you want to do?

 Survival Exercise: Think about what you would do if you lost two of your best customers. Make a plan to prevent it before it becomes a reality.

What do you know?

6. Studying ...
the First Discipline
of Knowledge.

"There are some young fellows who
apparently think salesmanship is a
thing that they will someday find
somewhere ready made."

— John H. Patterson

"You don't get great at sales in a day,
you get great at sales day by day."

— Jeffrey Gitomer

The difference between reading and studying is intensity, focus and
repetition. To master salesmanship, you must continually repeat messages
and practice by doing in order to master the principles and the
fundamentals that will lead to success. Studying is defined as the
continuing self-discipline to achieve sales greatness.

Think about how you learn: When you were in high
school or college, how did you study for exams? How did
you learn your material? Note cards? Study groups?
Reading? Being quizzed? Cram? Cheat? Take notes? Those
habits are still with you.

Did you study to be a salesman or did you just think it
would happen overnight? Selling is a science. An acquired
skill. The sales person who you thought was born to sell
painstakingly developed the traits and characteristics to do
so, and then went about learning and applying the science
of selling.

Selling is a learned skill, acquired by people with the attitude, aptitude, fortitude, desire, and persistence to succeed.

Have you got the desire to learn the skills needed to succeed?

 Exercise: Read about, study or listen to one new sales technique each day, and before the end of the day try that technique out at least once. By trying it you'll see the real world application of what you thought might work.

Bonus: If you do one technique a day, at the end of the year, you'll have 250 new techniques and still have your weekends free.

And at the end of 5 years, you'll be a world class expert.

7. Your Library is the Artesian Well of Knowledge.

"What a fine thing your brain is; your brain is a part of all it has met; hence, meet great men -- you can meet them in books."

— *How to Close a Sale-NCR*

"Formal education will earn you a living, self education will earn you a fortune."

— *Jim Rohn*

"You determine how much of a fortune you want to earn by how much you decide to self-educate."

— *Jeffrey Gitomer*

It's difficult to read books if you don't own them. A library full of success books gives you the opportunity to gain the wisdom of others if you just employ this one word: READ.

If you want to know the intimate thought-patterns of someone else, look at their library.

What they read usually determines how they think. If you decide to read about success, the odds are you will become successful. Your library is something to build upon to help you continue your studying.

John D. Rockefeller didn't use a library card. He endowed the library. Reason? He bought books and kept them instead of borrowing them for a week.

Books are not just for reading. They are also for reference.

People often say to me "I read that book."
People **rarely** say to me, "I use the principles of that book every day." If you own the book there is a possibility that you might go back and refer to the book for additional knowledge or clarification.

Where is your personal library? What books constitute your library? What books are you using?

Training doesn't get you to the top of your plateau. Education does. Training teaches you how. Education teaches you WHY. Think about reading: Start by reading books about things you love or are interested in. That will begin to create the habit. And the thirst for knowledge. Knowledge, like any other addiction, is a drug. Fifteen beers? Or fifteen books? One will get you to the men's room, the other will allow you to own the men's room. Dedication to life-long learning means reading and listening to something for your personal development at least an hour a day. Makes Sense!

Exercise: List the books you HAVE read that improved your sales game. Now, what book SHOULD you have read to improve your sales game? Ouch! Want the list? Go to www.gitomer.com and enter MAKE SENSE in the GitBit box.

More exercise: Read three books at once, a chapter at a time.

More, more exercise: Read two pages a day of a positive attitude book for the next 25 years.

Note of caution: Old personal development books (Hill, Marden, Carnegie) are hokey. BUT they are equally as valid. Idiots will pass them off as passé and not read them.

Don't be an idiot!

8. Planning Prevents Wandering and Provides Direction.

"If you plan your work you will not find yourself standing on the corner wondering where to go next."
                              — *John H. Patterson*

"Goals are the road map that will direct you to success."   — *Jeffrey Gitomer*

The same people who use road maps for traveling often omit road maps from succeeding.

A solid plan of attack for personal development, product knowledge, and market penetration will provide a faster, more successful result.

There's an old cliché that if Moses had a map he would not have had to wander for forty years.

Got map?

A personal mission statement is your affirmation, philosophy, and purpose rolled into one.

It's an opportunity to bring your goals into focus and transfer your ideals into the real world. It's a chance for you to write your own legacy. It's your personal challenge to yourself. Sounds pretty heavy, but actually it's fun if you do it right.

Do you write down your goals?
How many have you accomplished in the last month or year? What would help you meet your goals in the next 30 days? Six months? Or one year? Don't let your goals fall by the wayside (like your New Year's resolutions).

Exercise: Post-it Note your way to real achievement. Post-it note your goals on your bathroom mirror. Look at them until you are sick of looking at them, and then begin to achieve them. Once you achieve them put them on your bedroom mirror, so each day you can begin by looking at your success.

Another exercise: Direct yourself. Each day, create one single direction that you must achieve. Even if your ass falls off. Just one thing that at the end of each day you can say, "I did it!" After a month it will be easy to add one more thing. At the end of a year, you will be doing ten things a day and accomplishing them all.

Notice I did not say make a long term plan. I DID say take daily actions. If you take the right daily actions, the long term plans are automatically achieved. Long term goals can be overwhelming. Short daily directed actions are easily achieved. The secret is the "Daily Dose."

9. Use "Today Time Management."

"Nothing in business is as valuable as time."

> — *John H. Patterson*

"The successful person takes advantage of time, the unsuccessful person laments in the lack of it."

> — *Jeffrey Gitomer*

Every person has the same amount of time.

A wise investment of time is the best non-monetary investment you can make. Time management is intuitive for some, but it can also be a learned process.

The basic underlying principle of time management is "do what's important first."

Time management is not complicated -- unless you take a time management course. Then you have to have a minor degree in rocket science to figure out what piece of paper gets what notes in what category and with what priority.

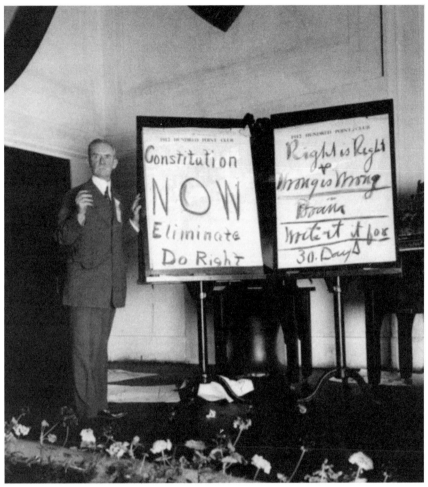

Patterson addressing the 100 Point Club, 1912.

"People do not realize the immense
value of utilizing spare minutes."
— *Orison Swett Marden*

"Turn off the TV at home -- It's pretty
much a waste of time. Invest your time
in reading a book."
— *Jeffrey Gitomer*

Create Post-it notes with the day's tasks. At the end of the day check them off. If you didn't accomplish any, you didn't have a productive day.

 Use your time wisely. Don't waste time with people that can't make the decision to purchase.

 Exercise: Get in front of people who can say Yes. This is the single highest priority and most productive use of your time. The time you spend face-to-face is in direct proportion to the number of sales you will make.

Want to double your sales?

Easy -- just double the time
you spend in front of people
who can say **Yes** to you.

10. Prospect for Probable Purchasers.

"Take it for granted that everyone can buy, rather than determining without an interview that some people will not buy."
— *John H. Patterson*

"Good fundamental sales skills and solid product knowledge are meaningless unless you see and follow-up the proper number of prospects."
— *Jeffrey Gitomer*

Every prospector was in search of a gold mine. "Gold fever," they called it. They would pay any amount of money for the map that would lead them to the gold. Many paid with their lives. Prospecting for probable purchasers is not as dangerous but is equally as rewarding. **How** to prospect is equally as important as **where** to prospect. Or better stated, proper prospecting prevents poverty.

Looking for new prospects? Who isn't? You probably have hundreds you're not paying attention to ... YOUR PRESENT CUSTOMERS! They already know you and like you, you have established rapport, confidence, and trust, you know they have good credit because they have paid you in the past, and you know they will return your call! I don't think you have to ask for much more than that. Beats cold calling!

With a few exceptions there is very little difference between one company and another, or one company's products or another's.

The following are the simple (but not easy) personal characteristics of why customers will buy from you. All of which you have probably heard before, but doing them AND believing them AND living them makes the difference!

Here are your personal mantras for finding probable purchasers:
I Work Hard. "Work only half a day. It makes no difference which half-the first 12 hours or the last 12 hours." – *Kemmons Wilson*
I bring Solid Value. Provide something of value that will benefit the PP that your competition cannot match.
I am Responsive. Try to always exceed your customers expectations in all contacts you may have with them. Customers want you to get to the point, and they want you to get there fast.
I am a Straight Shooter. Build a reputation as an honest person. Tell the truth and you don't have to worry about what you say coming back to haunt you.
I build a Great Reputation. Do the right things consistently and you will build a reputation that precedes you. Your reputation will make it easier for you to continue to work with your existing customers, and to prospect new customers. If you have a bad reputation, good luck getting rid of it!
I Listen to Understand. If you are not so busy doing all of the talking your customers in most cases will tell you exactly what they want and what you need to do to "get the business."
I Keep my Customers in Front of my Face. Keep your key customer list on your desk. If you have not spoken with one of them in a while pick up the phone before your competition does.
I Follow Through. Say what you will do, and do what you say you will do. Follow through develops reputation. So does dropped balls.
I Find their Comfort Zone. Once you get a customer in a comfort zone you have to screw up to lose them. Like an old shoe or favorite shirt, they will be reluctant to seek out alternatives as long as you "feel good." If they look elsewhere, look in the mirror as to why.
The most important reason my customers do business with me: I still ask for the business. Your customer wants to know that they continue to be important, and that you are still hungry.

 Exercise:
Call one customer a day and ask for their business.

11. Increase Business Connections to Increase Sales.

"A good plan is to have your agents assemble ... and have each one explain to you his methods of selling and the arguments he uses ... a convention of this sort will put dollars into your pocket."

— *John H. Patterson*

"Networking is creating momentum toward business and career success."

— *Jeffrey Gitomer*

Today it's called networking.

Patterson was a proponent of business people interacting with one another. Trade shows, conventions, business meetings, seminars, and business gatherings of all kinds.

Patterson was able to make sales in any social environment. From banquets to ballgames. From picnics to presidential retreats. He understood that business was not simply completed at a sales call or in an office, and that often his biggest deals were made in non-business environments or during atypical "business" hours.

Consider the
5 basic rules of networking.

1. Go where the probable purchasers are

2. Give first

3. Dig in

4. Be consistent

5. Get to know people on a friendly basis

How well do you do? How would you rate yourself, and more importantly, how would your COMPETITION rate you and rate themselves? Time to get in gear and get out there!

People tend to do business with people they trust.

Be sincere and **be yourself**.

Have breakfast, have dinner, have fun with your PP and you will build a basic platform upon which they will WANT to do business with YOU.

Exercise: List five places where your five best customers go. Go there.

12. Creating the Demand converts Selling to Buying.

"If the prospect understood the proposition, he would not have to be sold; he would come to buy."

— *John H. Patterson*

"People don't like to be sold, but they love to buy.™"

— *Jeffrey Gitomer*

John Patterson's objective was not to sell cash registers. Rather, **he created the demand for a receipt**.

He encouraged people at every possible moment to "ask for a receipt." This message reached people without cash registers and provoked thought in a manner that produced the desire to purchase his machines.

Desire leads to demand.

Create the need.
Prove the need.
Don't just sell the product.

Why do you buy personal objects? Is it a NEED, or a WANT?

Patterson was the first to understand that buying was an emotional process.

You must create a balance between the emotion to trigger the sale, and the logic to justify the purchase.

You've seen it at Christmas. Cabbage Patch dolls, Tickle Me Elmo stuffed toys. The latest craze. The average consumer can't get enough of it. That's demand. If you could do the same for your business it would be a much easier life than the one you've got.

Demand comes from desire.
Desire comes from perceived value or gain.

Exercise: List five values (not benefits) that a customer receives by purchasing from you. I'll bet you can't.

13. A Prepared Demonstration means Personalized!

"Don't go out shooting until you have your ammunition ready."

— *John H. Patterson*

"A fumbling, excuse-making, apologizing salesperson builds zero confidence."

— *Jeffrey Gitomer*

Most salespeople are only halfway prepared to give a sales presentation or sales demonstration. They know many things about themselves and not enough about how the PP (probable purchaser) profits from the use of their products.

This is not caused by lack of preparation, this is caused by lack of *proper* preparation.

NOTE: Failure does not come from lack of sales, failure comes from lack of preparation.

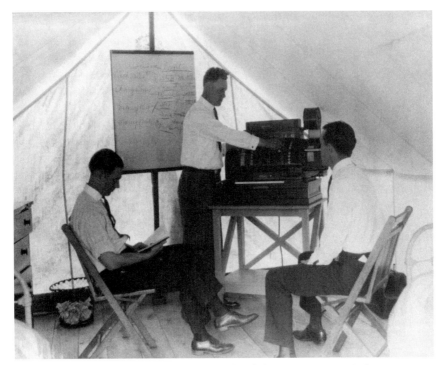

Sales agents practicing personalized demonstrations. c1925

"'Good enough' is the enemy of all progress."

— *John H. Patterson's favorite quote*

"If you don't personalize your sales presentation, you will lose to someone who does."

— *Jeffrey Gitomer*

Outcomes are predetermined if you prepare.

How well do prepare for your presentation? Do you know more than his or her name, title and the company name when you walk into the PP's office?

Before your next presentation, have a handle on these five statements:

1. I know who the probable purchaser is currently purchasing my product or service from.

2. I know whether the probable purchaser has sole authority to purchase from us or whether purchasing decisions are a committee decision.

3. I know whether anyone from my company has called on this probable purchaser before.

4. I know whether the probable purchaser ever bought from us before and, if so, why he or she didn't continue to purchase from us.

5. I know how my probable purchaser will profit from his purchase of my product.

Exercise: Learn to employ the rule of 50+50=50 … Spend 50% of your time preparing about how your customer will benefit. You will give a 50% better presentation, and you will walk away with 50% more business.

14. Gain Interest with Information about the PP not the We-We.

"Always leave him (the merchant) in such a frame of mind that he will be glad to have you call again."

— *John H. Patterson*

"Product knowledge is useless until you know how your product is used on the job to benefit and create profit for the customer."

— *Jeffrey Gitomer*

In order to arouse the interest of a probable purchaser, it is the responsibility of the salesperson to be interesting.

The best way to gain the interest of the PP is to share methods and strategies for profitability and productivity and save the boring (non-interesting) details for later.

How much talking does the PP do when you and he meet? How many PROFIT ideas are you bringing with you?

Remember that the probable purchaser is most interested in HIS benefit from buying your product or service.

Use the 'You' method, not the 'I' method.

Talk about your probable purchaser's interests rather than your own if you want to keep his attention.

The more you know about them, the easier it is to sell them. If you bring your knowledge about the PP and how they **profit from use** -- not how they save -- how they profit -- the more likely it is that they will buy from you.

Exercise: Videotape yourself giving a sales presentation. How many we-we phrases are you using? Are you boring your PP with drivel about your company? If someone were giving YOU this presentation, how long would it take for you to fall asleep?

Now count the number of times you specifically address the needs and concerns of the PP. Are you even connecting with them? Take note and take heart -- and change your presentation. It's got to be all about the PP, not the We-We.

15. Questions Lead to Answers. Answers Lead to Sales.

"Questions … may start a train of thought that will lead to good results."
— *John H. Patterson*

"Questions are the heart of the sale."
— *Jeffrey Gitomer*

In 1888, Sherlock Holmes stated "It is a capital offense to theorize before one has data." This was actually said by Arthur Conan Doyle on behalf of Holmes. Preparing the proper questions will lead to answers in which the prospective purchaser will convince himself that he is making the right decision to buy. The proper questions will lead to answers that bind potential profit with probable purchase.

What can the proper power questions do for you? Engage the probable purchaser and earn more sales!

Do you have 25 of them -- the most powerful questions you can create -- at your fingertips?

No? Join the crowd. 95% of all salespeople don't. That could be why only 5% of salespeople rise to the top. Just a theory (or is it?).

Here are the 7.5 questioning success strategies:

1. Ask the probable purchaser questions that make him evaluate new information.

2. Ask questions that qualify needs.

3. Ask questions about improved productivity, profits or savings.

4. Ask questions about company or personal goals.

5. Ask questions that separate you from your competition -- not compare you to them.

6. Ask questions that make the customer or probable purchaser think before giving a response.

7. Ask Power Questions to create a BUYING atmosphere -- not a selling one.

7.5 A critical success strategy: To enhance your listening skills, write down answers. It proves you care, preserves your data for follow-up, keeps the record straight, and makes the customer feel **important**.

Exercise: Ask the wrong questions, get the wrong answers. Here's the challenge: Get one probable purchaser or customer to say, "No one ever asked me that before."

16. Listening Leads to Understanding.

"Don't talk for the sake of talking."
— *John H Patterson*

"Listening is one of the most important aspects of the selling process, yet it's usually the weakest part of a sales professional's skill set."
— *Jeffrey Gitomer*

There are two basic kinds of listening: listening with the intent to respond and listening with the intent to understand.

Listening with intent to respond leads to interruption. This lesson focuses on the science of using both disciplines in the order of understanding FIRST, and responding SECOND.

Here's a two word lesson on listening -- it's the only/best way to be certain your listening skills are as good as your selling skills. And those two words are not "shut up!" The two words are: **take notes**.

Note taking makes listening a certainty,
and lets the customer know his words
are valuable enough to write down.

Are you a talker or a listener?
Learn to be as good at shutting up as you are at talking.

When you leave a meeting, does your recollection of a meeting ever differ from the person that was sitting right next to you? Maybe it's because you were distracted -- most likely it's because you didn't take notes.

Ever catch yourself formulating the next words to come out of your mouth rather than listening to the person until they were done speaking? Sure you have -- it's human nature. Don't do that.

Here's a method toward error free positive communication ...

1. Focus eye contact on the communicator.

2. Write the communication down.

3. Repeat it back or ask about it.

4. Get confirmation.

4.5 Deliver what you promised.

Exercise: LEARN how to be a better listener by asking a question at the end of their statement. If you make a statement, it's possible that you were interrupting. But with a question, you almost HAVE to wait until they're finished speaking.

17. Less Sell-Talk Time Leads to More Buy-Time.

"Don't talk all the time.
Give the merchant a chance."
— *John H. Patterson*

"If you listen better you will sell more."
— *Jeffrey Gitomer*

The balance between letting the PP talk and the salesman talk must be weighed heavily in favor of the PP. Most salespeople make the fatal mistake of selling when in fact the more the PP talks, the more they will sell themselves on the product or service.

The salesman's responsibility is to create ways to let the PP have more talk time. This is done through powerful questioning. The more powerful the question, the more "probable purchaser" becomes "profitable customer."

Salespeople think they have to "sell" to make the sale, and nothing could be further from the truth. If you let the customer talk long enough, they will see the purpose and value of saying yes. They will sell themselves.

Questions and listening go hand in hand.

The only person who loses by having poor listening skills is you! How are you listening? Do you know how and when to be quiet? You can learn a lot from your PP if you give them the chance to talk!

Look for these two symptoms of lousy listeners:

A person who seems to have all the answers usually isn't listening.

A person who interrupts isn't listening (or at least is not a good listener).

Exercise: Ask every customer a two-part question that when answered would be a reason to buy. First ask what their experience has been. Let them talk. Then ask why they are buying now, and what they hope to gain as a result of purchase.

This exercise will give the PP maximum talk time -- and give you maximum understanding of their situation.

18. Your message must be as compelling as your product to engage the PP.

"You interest people, first, by the thing you talk about; and second, by the way you talk."

— *Manual for N.C.R. Salesmen*

"The secret to sales is not just engagement, it is *INTELLIGENT* Engagement."

— *Jeffrey Gitomer*

The key to any sale rests in how well you engage the prospect.

If you engage the prospect, you create an atmosphere to buy.
If you not only engage at the beginning, but also at the end of the meeting, the prospect is eager to buy.

Your preparation, the questions you ask, the ideas you bring, your communication and presentation skills, and your positive attitude and enthusiasm are the keys to intelligent engagement.

An engaging question is one that makes the person stop and think, and respond in terms of you.

What is the most engaging question in the world?...
Will you Marry Me?

Will you marry me is a question about the PP, that makes them stop and think, and respond in terms of you. What is your 'Will you marry me' question? Do you have one? How much of a commitment do your PP's make when they answer your questions?

 Real engagement is the most difficult part of selling because the salesperson (you) is unprepared to engage. Oh, you may be prepared to sell, (crap about you and your product) -- but you are ill prepared to engage (stuff about the customer and how he profits from purchase). Create five great engagement questions.

 Exercise: Substitute television with sales call preparation. Give up TV for two nights a week, and just prepare questions that will engage the prospect, gather valuable information, and ask for the sale. I promise you it will put more money in your pocket than watching your favorite show.

19. An Objection is the Gateway to a Sale.

"An objection is nearly always
an advantage to the salesman ...
to turn the objection into a real
reason for buying."

— *John H. Patterson*

"The sale starts when the customer
objects."   — *Jeffrey Gitomer*

When a PP objects, protests, rejects, or denies, he is giving a signal that he does not believe in or trust in you, the product, or the company and that more information is needed. If you become deflated when you hear an objection, it is likely you may not make many sales. This is a curable condition once you understand the PP's cues.

Objections actually indicate interest
and the need for more clarification
or more proof on the part of the PP,
and the salesperson's responsibility
is to provide it enthusiastically.

Look forward to objections.
They are the gateway to a sale.

If you can overcome an objection in your presentation before the prospect raises it, you are more likely to make a sale.

Major clue ...
an objection may actually indicate purchaser interest!

7 steps to identify the true objection and learn how to overcome it:

1. Listen to the objection and decide if it's true.

2. Qualify it as the only one.

3. Confirm it again in a different way.

4. Qualify the objection to set up the close.

5. Answer the objection so that it completely resolves the issue and confirms the resolve.

6. Ask a closing question or communicate to the prospect in an assumptive (I have the sale in hand) manner.

7. Confirm the answer and the sale in writing.

Exercise: Create five answers for your biggest objections. You know they're coming, why not be ready to answer them in a creative way?

20. Selling is Not Manipulating, Selling is Harmonizing.

"The successful salesman must learn to be all things to all people."

— John H. Patterson

"Understand how your product is used (not just what it does) so you can understand how to harmonize with your prospect, and sell it most effectively."

— Jeffrey Gitomer

Selling is about understanding the other person. Each person has different motives to buy based on personality and needs. Salesmen can not give the same presentation all the time. You've got to adapt the presentation to meet the needs and the personality of the PP. Patterson changed the register models presented to fit the PP's personality type, not just their business type. This innovation made the product seem custom fit for the purchaser.

I'm against systems of selling. They teach you a way. Usually a manipulative way. And you gotta use that way. Problem is, prospects may not want to buy that way. Which way do you sell?

Harmony is understanding, sensing the tone and comfort level of the prospect.

As a SalesMaster, your job is to take the characteristics of the prospect and blend them with the reason the prospect is buying so that it motivates the prospect to act. And gives the prospect enough confidence to buy.

Think of harmony in music. Think of it the same way in sales.

Are you in sync with your PP? Are you in-tune or off-key?

Here are a few guidelines that will work on any type of purchaser:

1. Never argue.

2. Never offend.

3. Never think or act like you are defeated.

4. Try to make a friend at all costs.

5. Try to get on the same side of the fence (harmonize).

5.5 Never have to remember what you said (A. write it down. B. don't lie.)

Exercise: Write down the last five conflicts you had with a PP during a sale. Write down how you could have avoided them.

Try them the next time the same conflict-situation arises.

21. Complete the Sale with an Agreement to Buy ... and Be Certain to Give Them a Receipt.

"Closing the sale is getting the prospect's decision to buy."

— *John H. Patterson*

"Assume the sale."

— *Jeffrey Gitomer*

Most salespeople are willing to walk away from a sales situation without an answer regarding the PP's intent to purchase. The true PP will have no objection to being asked to purchase. Many times a salesperson is in the middle of a selling cycle and even here the sale must be asked for. You must always ask to confirm the next step in the cycle of selling. Refer to it as the principle of "one YES leads to another."

Patterson had it right.
It's not "closing" the sale,
it's "completing" the sale.
Huge difference.
Closing is pushing.
Completing is the last step
in the process of buying.

How do you complete the sale?
What is your selling cycle time?
What could you do to make it shorter?

Do that! How many meetings/presentations/phone calls does it take you to close the sale? And, remember, you are a SALESperson and the PP is EXPECTING you to ask for the sale. Don't disappoint him.

The close is a delicate balance between your words and actions and the PP's thoughts and perceptions. Your objective is to get the PP to think "ownership."

Exercise: Start by looking at your last five sales. How did they happen? How did you complete them? Now make a plan to incorporate those strategies into every presentation and every sales cycle.

Success in sales is repeatable, if you learn from your successes.

22. Service is the Reputation for the Next Sale.

"Quality in selling starts with service."
— *John H. Patterson*

"Your friendliness and willingness
to help is in direct proportion to
your success."
— *Jeffrey Gitomer*

"To serve is to rule" is a 5,000 year-old Chinese proverb. The more a salesperson learns that service is the biggest part of the sale, the more his reputation will grow as an honest, ethical, helpful, and sincere businessperson worthy of repeat business and a referral.

All customers need service. The big question is: How do you respond?

Why do some of your customers
love you and some hate you?

Why do some stay loyal and some leave?

What can you do to make
your service memorable?

What are you doing to maintain
real customer loyalty?

Loyal is the most difficult of the customer service goals to achieve. But once you have it, you have something your competition will never have -- the next order. Give solutions, not excuses. That is what customers want.

Exercise: Call five customers at random, and ask them about how they feel about doing business with you. Ask them why they would do business with you again.

Then call your five best customers, and ask them why they will do business with you again. Then call five customers you lost and find out why you lost them.

Those twenty answers, when combined and studied, will give you the answers you need to grow and prosper with a combination of new customers and well retained old customers.

23. Extra Service Leads to the "Testimonial Word."

"Give them that little extra service which keeps customers pleased ... remember, a satisfied user is the best advertisement you can have."

— *John H. Patterson*

"Exceptional service lowers the barriers to testimonial sales."

— *Jeffrey Gitomer*

All customers expect great service. Very few get it. What happens from the time the sale is made until the next purchase is about to be made, determines who gets the next order. The "service" part of the relationship you have with your customers determines your fate for future business.

Your biggest job is not to sell. Your biggest job is to deliver MEMORABLE service.

Going beyond what is expected means surprising, anticipating, delighting, and even rescuing the customer at a precise moment in time. Consistently going beyond what is expected leads to stories and referrals. It's also known as word-of-mouth advertising.

Your customers can be walking, talking testimonials.

When you are done speaking with a customer or the transaction is over, that is when they START talking. They will say one of three things ... something good, nothing, or something bad ... and the cool part is you choose by the way you act around them, and the way you treat them. How are you treating your customers? What are your customers saying about you?

Facts and figures are forgotten but stories are retold again and again. Exceptional service lowers the barrier to testimonial sales. If you have created exceptional opportunities for your customer, they will be more than happy to tell their story to the media and to other perspective customers.

You don't need permission from a boss to make a customer feel great.

Think about a time when you felt good because you had good service. Make someone else feel that good feeling.

Pick out one customer every day and make them feel great!

Here are your possibilities as you look at the service process: Your customer *MAY* come back if the product was good and the service was acceptable (this is satisfied). Your customer *WILL* come back if the product was great (this is loyal). Your customer *WILL COME BACK **AND TELL OTHERS*** if the product was the greatest, and the service was memorable (that is the definition of loyal, testimonial, and referral).

Exercise: Look at your last five referrals. How did they come about? Measure how many unsolicited referrals you get each week. Five should be a minimum number. Then create a game plan of what you can do EVERY DAY that the customer would consider memorable, and do that.

Customer service
is not about who's right or wrong.
It's about how you react to,
respond, and handle the problem.

24. Referrals are Better Earned than Asked For.

"Satisfied users are always your best advertisement, and the more of them you have in your territory the more money you will make."

— *John H. Patterson*

"A referral is the easiest sale to make."

— *Jeffrey Gitomer*

There are two basic types of referrals. Solicited and unsolicited. A solicited referral is one that you ask for. Unsolicited referrals are the ones that you earn. There are two basic forms of unsolicited referrals: customer driven and PP driven. Unsolicited referrals are like a business report card -- it will tell you how well you are performing in the marketplace. You will ONLY get an unsolicited referral when you are at the highest level of market performance.

The definition of referral is **risk**.

The definition of a referral is risk, because someone is willing to risk their friendship or relationship with another to have them contact you for a purchase. People are only willing to risk when they are confident and comfortable that the risk is low and the possible rewards are so high that they outweigh any hesitancy in giving the referral.

Are you willing to refer your clients or customers to someone else? Is someone else willing to refer their clients or customers to you? Answer: Yes, if there is mutual trust.

You could double your business if you got every one of your present customers to refer ONE more customer just like themselves.

If you can't call, or have a hard time calling on your present customer, or if you come up with some lame excuse like, "I've sold them everything I can sell them," it really means:

> — You have failed to establish enough rapport with the customer.

> — You have probably not followed up well (or at all) after the sale.

> — Your customer had some problem and you are reluctant to call and open a can of worms.

> — You are in need of more training.

> — And the big one…you have not developed a proper relationship with the customer.

I am constantly amazed at the sales people who make sales and move to the next prospect.

I challenge you to look at your
customer list carefully and honestly.
I'll bet there are hundreds
of opportunities to sell **something**.

 Exercise: List your five biggest customers. List your five best customers (relationship wise). Are they the same? They better be or you're in trouble. If not, stop here and develop a game plan to make than happen within one year.

More exercise: List five ways you can earn a referral.

More, more exercise: Make a game plan to implement each referral strategy.

25. Testimonials Will Sell When the Salesman Can't.

"Overcome objections with
testimonials."

— *John H. Patterson*

"One testimonial has more strength
than a hundred presentations."

— *Jeffrey Gitomer*

When a salesperson speaks of himself, his company, or his product, he is either selling or bragging or both. When a loyal customer speaks on behalf of the product in the form of a testimonial, it is proof, and in fact, it is the only proof that a salesperson has to substantiate his claims. If a customer is on the fence and is choosing between one company and another, it is the testimonial, not the salesperson, which will sway the decision.

Testimonials, like referrals, are report cards. If you are having trouble getting them, that's not a problem ... that's a symptom. And you better look deeper into your method of doing business or your products capability to find the answer. Most salespeople mistakenly blame the customer when they can't get a referral or testimonial. Big mistake.

Testimonials are PROOF -- and they're the only proof you've got.

When is the right time to ask for a testimonial?

Not sure? That might be the reason you don't have as many as you would like. You may be asking at the wrong time or asking the wrong people.

Do you have a notebook full of testimonial letters categorized by topic to show your PP? Don't lay them all out at once -- be sure to pull the right one at the right time, or else it won't work! You must pull the right testimonials that pertain specifically to their objections. Isn't it about time to put your testimonials into 21st century technology? Isn't a video more powerful than a letter?

Exercise: Select your five BEST customers. The ones who really love you. Make an appointment to see them for a testimonial. A VIDEO testimonial. Live recordings of what they think of you.

If you only do ONE THING from the entire book, do this.

A collection of video testimonials will go further than any other sales tool times ten.

Do a video testimonial CD and the world is your sales oyster.
If you just use letters, you're just like every other clam.

26. Advertising Brings Awareness. Testimonial Advertising Brings Customers.

"A satisfied user is the best advertisement you could have."

— *John Patterson*

"Word of mouth advertising is fifty times more powerful than advertising."

— *Jeffrey Gitomer*

Everyone wants to be well-known. Everyone wants to be a household word. Everyone wants to be perceived as a leader. And everyone makes the mistake of tooting their own horn in an ad. One third-party endorsement is worth a hundred self-praising ads.

Testimonials are sales power.

A testimonial ad creates 4.5 winning situations.

1. It provides proof that your product is what you say it is.

2. It strengthens the loyalty bond between you and the customer in the ad.

3. It's the only proof you've got.

4. It reduces the risk of purchasing.

4.5 It deflates the competition (especially if it is a testimonial of a customer who switched).

Testimonial ad that appeared May 21, 1947.

"Testimonials are proof that your claims are true."

— John H. Patterson

"Customers are the most powerful salespeople on your team."

— Jeffrey Gitomer

Who are your five best customers?

How did they choose you?

Did they switch from a competitor?

Do they find value in your services beyond your price?

Will they do a testimonial for you?

If you can create an army of people talking about you, instead of a bunch of self-righteous drivel about "we're the greatest," you'll make more sales than you ever dreamed. The question is do you have an army of people who love you enough to spread the word?

Exercise: Create a video testimonial for every aspect of your selling process. Work them into your sales presentation at the appropriate times. Watch your sales increase.

Testimonials are more powerful than salespeople.

27. If You Have Done Your Homework and Prepared Well, It Will Be Evident in Your Sales Report Card.

"Remember, the demonstration has but one object, the sale of the register. No matter how well you think you have demonstrated the register, if you do not close the sale, you have failed in your purpose."

— *John H. Patterson*

"Weak sales people look at quotas and become fearful. Mediocre sales people look as quotas as a goal. Great sales people look at quotas and laugh."

— *Jeffrey Gitomer*

Patterson established the first quota system used. When he established the system, it was a relative number based on the salesman's territory. It was a reflection of what the salesman should be able to bring in based upon the wealth of his territory. Back then and still today, quotas are a system to measure the **minimum** standard of achievement.

Here's a rule I created. It's called: The Rule of **The More The More**: The more you believe the more you will sell. The more value you provide to others, the more people will come to know and respect you. The more you study sales, the more you will know how to react to any sales situation. The more you cold call, the more you will know how to master the science of thinking and responding creatively. The more you follow up, the more sales you will make.

Reach GOALS not quotas.
Think being BEST not quotas.

What is keeping you from reaching your quota? Reaching goals? Being the best?

If you execute the fundamentals to the BEST of your ability, goals get met, and quotas get blown away.

Exercise: List the five fundamental things you need to do every day that will assure that you make a sale. Repeat them each day no matter what.

28. Competition Means Prepare to Be Your Best.

"Treat competition fairly."

— John H. Patterson

"Competition does not mean war.
It means learn, it means prepare,
and it means be your best."

— Jeffrey Gitomer

Competitors want the business just as much as you do. They will fight, they will undercut, they will play dirty, and they will go to any length to prevent you from getting the sale. Your job is to get the sale and maintain your highest standard of doing business. This can be accomplished by out-thinking and out-performing the competition. And you have thousands of people who will help you at any moment in time. You know them ... they are your own loyal customers.

Here are two ways to address the competition:

1. Go "over" the competition. The ideal way to win. It assumes that you take the high ground. It doesn't mean sit back and wait. It means rise above in a way that the competition has to respond or lose. Here are a few "over" ways. Ezine. Seminars. Referrals. Build value by building profit. Earn testimonials and use them to get "over" again.

More "over". Others speaking on your behalf is better than any sales pitch "against" someone else. I'll make you one promise: if you invest the time and effort it takes to go "over" the competition, you will be rewarded beyond your wildest dreams, AND sales will be easier and more fun.

And once you reach a high level of "**over**" you will be qualified for the highest level...

2. Ignore the competition. I have spent the last ten years ignoring the competition. Building my presentation skills and writing skills. Competitors read my weekly article in their hometown. They hate me, and I love it.

Do I know them? Some. Most I don't. Sales and competition share the same adage. "It's not who you know, it's who knows you." Sounds a bit stuffy, but let me assure you that it's better to build your skills than try to "beat" someone.

I go for "best" not "beat." It's a better, cleaner win. Do I always win? No. But I always feel I should have. And I have a self-confidence that keeps me ready for the next opportunity. And I wake up the next day and go to work sharpening my skills.

My ways of dealing with my competition (over or ignore) are the hardest ways – but they work. And the longer you go "over" them the more you can ignore them.

Yes, I want to beat the crap out of the competition -- it's instinctive. But a smarter path is to have them looking over their shoulders to see where you are. Let them "hear-your-footsteps" and beat them by being "chosen" or "preferred."

How many ways are there to deal with the competition?

How do you deal with them?
What do you say about them?
How do you beat them?
How often do you beat them?

The goal is to separate yourself from the competition and from everyone else. Have creative, new ideas; have the sale in finished form (design done, preliminary layout, sample); have a WOW multimedia presentation; have a comparison chart of key areas where you beat the competition. Got boring business cards? Get new ones made, even if it's out of your own pocket.

IMPORTANT NOTE: Don't down the competition. If you have nothing nice to say, say nothing. This is a tempting rule to break ... the sirens are sweetly singing. Set yourself apart from them with preparation and creativity. Don't slam them. Downing the competition is not a no-win situation; it's an absolute losing situation.

When a prospect picks you over the competition, it's a day to celebrate -- and a day to discover "why" -- when you figure out why you were chosen, all you have to do is repeat the process.

Do things (professionally) no one else would do.

 Exercise: Look at your last five sales where you were chosen over the competition. Write down the primary factors of why you won.

Now do the same thing for losses. Look at your last five sales that you LOST to the competition. Write down the primary factors of WHY you lost.

Now all you have to do is strengthen the reasons why you were chosen and fix the reasons you weren't and PRESTO! more sales -- And you can thank the competition for them. Cool.

29. Recognize and Thank Those Who Have Helped You Succeed.

"People seldom improve themselves when they have no other model but themselves to look after."

— *John H. Patterson*

"The game of selling is a TEAM sport, not an individual sport."

— *Jeffrey Gitomer*

"I'd like to thank the members of the academy ..." Don't forget to say thank you to those that helped you along the way. This is true not only if you are a salesperson, this is true for the corporate executives that still have their own washroom and private cafeteria.

Patterson did a tremendous job thanking not only his sales team but ALL of his employees. From rewards through the still existing "100 Point Club," to factory improvements, rewards and incentives, Patterson did his best to reward and satisfy each salesman's need for appreciation.

You need co-workers to help you succeed. All at different levels of career achievement. The boss can help you, and so can the truck driver. And most times the lower level people are the most help. Acknowledge them. Thank them. Reward them. Let them know you care and are grateful for their help.

The Universal Thank You ...
Notice that you will always see
the words **"Thank You!"** on each and
every receipt you are given.

You didn't become a success on your own. And it didn't happen overnight. You may have even been lucky enough to have a mentor.

Take the time to acknowledge the people who have helped you succeed. Some will be readily apparent, but others may have seemed to have been against you when they were just trying to help you help yourself. Learn to discern the difference and thank them ALL.

Exercise: List five people you want to thank or acknowledge. Get a small gift of remembrance for them. I give autographed books. Go to www.executivebooks.com and buy the set of books by Charlie Tremendous Jones. If you request autographed copies he will sign them all at no additional cost. I keep a dozen for gifts.

Bonus exercise: Become a mentor to someone who can benefit from your experience and will appreciate your gift of wisdom. Having a mentor is a gift, and can make a world of difference to the person you've invested in. Pass it on.

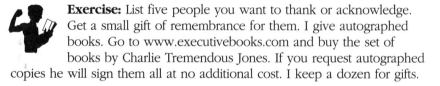

Thank You!

30. To Get Loyalty, You Must GIVE Loyalty.

"If its only money you get out of your job, you don't get enough."

— *John H. Patterson*

"Customer loyalty is the highest level of business achievement."

— *Jeffrey Gitomer*

Patterson wrote: Believe in your goods. Be loyal to your Company. Put your heart in your work. He wrote those words in 1889.

Gitomer's four pillars of loyalty are:
I. Loyalty to your company
II. Loyalty to your product
III. Loyalty to your customer
IV. Loyalty to yourself

Patterson's words and the four pillars of loyalty are the foundation for building long term business success.

Foundations of all buildings and houses start with pillars. Without the proper foundation, you have an unstable building, and an unstable customer.

It is the same in sales. If you don't have the four pillars of loyalty, your sales foundation is shaky.

 You must have the loyalty to all four parts.
If you aren't loyal to your company, you need to find a job/company/product you are loyal to.

 Exercise: List your five MOST loyal customers. Now list the reasons each one is loyal to you. Make a plan to instill those reasons in every one of your customers.

31. Exercise Must Be Both Physical and Mental.

"Ill health affects the mental ability; spoils the disposition, and handicaps one's progress."

— John H. Patterson

"Your physical status may be robbing you of a chance for fiscal sales success."

— Jeffrey Gitomer

You exercise your mind every day with new knowledge, both personal and professional. Unfortunately, most people don't exercise the rest of their body as consistently as they exercise their brain. Physical exercise is a perfect way to look great, feel great, act great, and think the greatest.

If exercise (either physical or mental) is lacking in your daily routine, it will show through on the outside (physical appearance) and on the inside (mental attitude).

There is a link between physical and mental fitness. Blood flow to the brain caused by physical exercise leads to clearer thoughts and better decisions.

NCR sales agents training class, July 11, 1924.
Can you imagine your sales team out in the field doing this? For a week? In the rain?

"People could not work at their best
unless their health was of the best."
— *John H. Patterson*

"Looking successful, is a big part of
achieving success. It starts with the
look of health."   — *Jeffrey Gitomer*

Have you ever noticed that some people just look more alive than others? In my experience I have found that people who combine physical and mental exercise seem more alert and ready to sell and serve. And by coincidence also seem to be the ones who can make their enthusiasm and self-confidence contagious.

Customers seem to receive healthy salespeople and their information in a more positive manner. I guess you could refer to it as the total package of brains, brawn, and beauty. And that equates to believability and buying from the probable purchaser.

> "Selling is a blend of mental and physical symphonic motions that perform in harmony with each other. When your mind and body aren't working in unison, the performance is off key."
>
> — *Jeffrey Gitomer*

Working-out can improve your business game. Sweat a little. Regular physical exercise can ... Reduce your level of anxiety. Help you manage stress more effectively. Improve your positive self-esteem and confidence. Help you relax. Help you sleep more restfully. And ... can teach you about goal-setting, dedication, and personal achievement.

Exercise: How can you NOT find 30 minutes 5 times a week to fit all those physical benefits into your mental sales plan?

32. Training is an Every Day Occurrence.

"Business is nothing but teaching."
— *John H. Patterson*

"Invest time, don't spend it. Training takes time. But it's the best life-long investment a person can make. Invest time in training."
— *Jeffrey Gitomer*

The word "training" is a misnomer. It's actually personal development and knowledge expansion. Education. Awareness. And the dedication to want to learn.

On-the-job training is one of the most important facets of a successful company. It must be real-time, in-depth, and contain thorough information tailored to each and every employee's personal learning styles. This way you are sure to maximize and retain the information. You never stop learning, so why should you stop training to be your best? Top athletes are constantly training to perfect their game, and stay at peak performance. Top salesmen need to do the same.

If you want to build wealth, first build a wealth of knowledge!

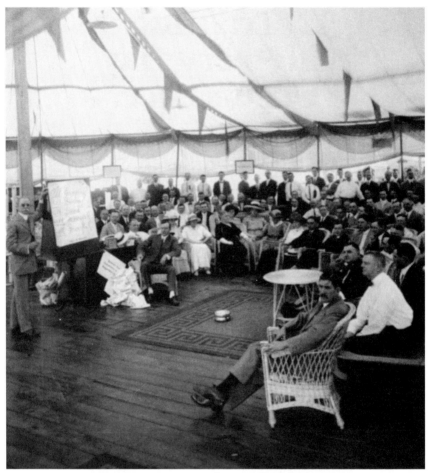

Patterson presenting to the "I Will" club in 1913.

"The best way to teach is through the eye. It is hard to retain what we hear, but a man remembers what he sees."

— *John H. Patterson*

"If you want to be great, learn how to get there."

— *Jeffrey Gitomer*

Are you spending or investing your time?

How many hours a day do you spend in front of the television? How is that helping your success? What is going to help your success more ... watching 30 minutes of re-runs, or dedicating 30 minutes to reading a book that will help the most important person in the world ... YOU!

Help yourself first! If your company does not have adequate training, create your own plan. All the information you need to succeed beyond your wildest dream already exists. The problem is, you're not exposing yourself to it.

Exercise: Self test AND game plan

— Do I spend 15 minutes a day reading or listening to sales information?

— Do I know how other people's jobs at my office affect my job and my performance?

— Do I read the trade magazines of our company's industry and the trade magazines of our top 5 customers' industries?

— Do I attend our industry's annual trade show?

— Do I belong to Toastmasters?

— Where's your training "road map" taking you?

33. Decide...
It Doesn't Matter If
It's Right or Wrong...
Decide!

"An executive is a man who decides.
Sometimes he decides right. But he
always decides."   *— John H. Patterson*

"If you want to succeed, you have to
fail a few times."   *— Max Gitomer (father)*

This was Patterson's way of saying "Take a risk, take a chance." Patterson's
whole life was risk and chance. He made decisions that risked his last
dime.

Patterson didn't take risks, he took calculated risks.

Patterson himself was a decision maker and he demanded the same out of
his executives. He could tolerate employees who made mistakes, but had
no patience with men who feared or hesitated to make a decision.

Decision making came quite easy to Patterson for the simple fact that he
had the instinctive and inveterate habit of analyzing situations realistically
instead of nominally. Patterson would reach a decision, no matter how
important or menial, by using his famous pyramid chart. Patterson even
went as far as standardizing this chart for his sales team.

The objective needing to be reached (the decision) would be at the apex
of the pyramid. Then he added a realistic analysis of the means by which
the objective might be attained. He standardized this method of decision
making throughout the organization so it came habitual for all employees
in the company to use when a decision needed to be reached. Patterson
wanted all his men to think alike, or at least like him. The pyramid chart
was the visual symbol of this. (See a pyramid chart in the hand of
Patterson himself on the next page.)

This pyramid chart was drawn by Patterson on the back page of a book on longevity. Patterson was inspired by reading, and took immediate action to write down ideas, concepts, and thoughts.

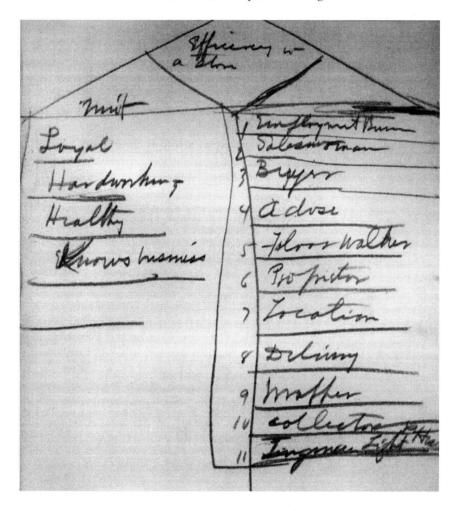

"It's not a matter of 'can't' decide.
It's a matter of 'won't' decide.
Can't means won't."

— *Jeffrey Gitomer*

Think about the last few decisions you delayed.

Why did you? Uncertainty? Timing not "right"? Not wanting to take the risk? You can always change the direction you are going, but not if you are standing still.

Postponing decision comes from lack of information.
Postponing decision comes from lack of factual information to make a sound judgment. Postponing decision comes from confusion or disorganization. Postponing decision comes from doubt or fear.

NOTE: Monday morning quarterbacks are the best non-decision makers in the world. They look at someone who took a risk, decided incorrectly, and now here you come saying "well, that's not what I would have done!" As you sit with your beer on your chickens nest, yelling at the TV.

How do you come to decisions?
Is it systematic? Or feeling?
Can't make decisions?
Try to use Patterson's way …
the Pyramid Chart.

Exercise: Make a pyramid chart for yourself. Start with a decision you'll have to make soon. Refer to the Patterson definitions and examples. Often when you write out the possibilities, the right decision becomes obvious.

34. You Become Known by the Actions You Take. Take Ethical Actions.

"There was a time when all successful salesmen were liars. That time has passed."
 — *John H. Patterson*

"You are more known for your deeds and your actions than for your words."
 — *Jeffrey Gitomer*

What is ethical? Who decides?

Use the 5-question acid test during the presentation ...

1. Is this in the best long-term interest of the customer?

2. Is this in the best long-term interest of my company?

3. Is this in the best long-term interest of my career?

4. If I were the prospect, would I buy?

5. Is it something that would make my mother proud?

These 5 questions are at the heart of ethics in the selling process. They must be asked every time a sale is being proposed.

Patterson knew 100 years ago the importance of ethics in business, and wanted his men to portray a trusting, pleasing, and earnest image.

My experience has shown me that if you have to say what you are, you probably aren't.

Think about that for a moment. "I'm honest," "I'm ethical," -- even "I'm the decision-maker," "I'm the boss," or "I'm in charge," usually indicates just the opposite. Doesn't it?

There's an easy way to measure the results of your ethics ...

• Can you sell the same customer again?

• Has the customer referred you another customer -- without being asked to do so? Get proof of your ethics, get better, or get out.

Exercise: The challenge is for you to rededicate yourself to helping or to satisfying the needs of the customer or prospect each time you sell. Your words and actions must be in harmony with the prospect's thoughts and perceptions in order to establish a comfort level that motivates the prospect to buy.

How do you achieve PP comfort level? You have to believe in it, you have to practice it, and you have to show your beliefs with deeds and ethical actions -- every day.

34.5 If it has been working for 100 years or more don't even think about changing it.

"There is nothing new under the sun but there are lots of old things we don't know."

— *Ambrose Bierce*

"If you want to learn something new or get a new idea, read a book that's 70 years old."

— *Jeffrey Gitomer*

Tradition is everywhere. Football rivalries that go back over 100 years. Democrats vs Republicans, any religious ceremony, holidays, and parades. And people are attracted to, and attracted by tradition. They fly thousands of miles to participate. They talk about it. They compare it to last year or years gone by. Patterson's principles, strategies, and ideas are no different.

Tradition is a sacred, powerful, insurance of success.

CPC parade in downtown Dayton in the snow, c1920.

"Reward those who have helped you succeed with a public display of appreciation."

— *John H. Patterson*

"People will try to rain on your parade because they have no parade of their own."

— *Jeffrey Gitomer*

The Tradition of The 100 Point Club

The 100 Point Club (now the Century Point Club) was started for salesmen who sold 100 points per month. Each register was appointed a specific point value. To qualify, any salesmen in the NCR American Selling Force who secured 100 points per month anytime after January 1, 1906 qualified as a member. The insignia of this exclusive club is a solitaire diamond mounted on a solid gold star; the star being emblematic of the high standard of salesmanship, and the gem of the quality of his ability. This club still meets nearly 100 years later. That's tradition.

CPC convention, 1920.
John Patterson front row, second from right.

The benefit was an all expense paid two-week convention in Ohio with the officers of the company. Patterson started dangling hefty rewards for those who exceeded their sales goals. Some rewards were as large and grand as a new car. Every reward was carefully calculated to grasp the desire of the salesman. Only merchandise of the highest quality was given. All NCR salesmen were working for something beyond salary and commission. They had something extra to strive for, in turn producing a hard working, goal-achieving and dedicated salesman.

Loyalty Produces Leaders was the motto adopted by the members of the 100 Point Club during their first annual convention. This motto explains how the men who attended the convention gained the high honor of being the leaders of the American selling force.

The 100 Pointers are loyal

1. To their Company

2. To their Company's methods

3. To their own ideas of high class salesmanship

4. To good business practice

The 100 Point Club was a celebration, an acknowledgement, and a learning experience. Almost one hundred years later, the 100 Point Club is still alive. Very alive.

I have had the privilege and the honor of addressing that group at their convention. It was a thrill and a challenge to do my part of providing new knowledge.

Traditions are a valuable asset and a link to success. They link the past with the present. They help you see what has been done. They help you remember what to do. And they give you the confidence you can do it, because it's been done before.

Traditions are there for you to learn from and embrace. They are there to help you succeed.

THE LEGEND OF THE 1904 WORLD'S FAIR

NCR exhibit at the 1904 World's Fair in St. Louis.

NCR had an exhibit at the 1904 World's Fair. John Patterson was shrewd enough to convince every concessionaire to purchase a cash register and issue receipts for purchases. This ensured Patterson ultimate exposure for his machines throughout the fair.

Every exhibitor was emphatic about visitors not touching their wares. "Do not touch" signs were everywhere -- except at the NCR exhibit. Patterson invited everyone to "touch." He encouraged people to try the machines and print receipts for themselves.

These actions are more proof of Patterson's winning sales strategies.

How to Live
THE PRINCIPLES

It's easy to read the principles and commit them to memory. It's easy to read these principles and say to yourself, "Yeah, I already know that." But that isn't *living* these principles. To live is to incorporate them into your life. They worked 100 years ago, and they still work today.

NOTE: Patterson was not distracted by a TV. Rather, he was distracted with family and books. To understand the Patterson model of success, it may be necessary to avoid or ignore the television for some period of time.

With each principle there is an exercise. By taking action you are learning to live the principle. However, you can't just do them, you must master them. Master the actions and then you will live the principles to their fullest. It will take some time, and a great deal of self-discipline, but the end result will be profitable in more ways than you can imagine. Not just in sales. In life.

Please also note that I didn't say "do" the Principles, I said "live" them. Exercise is combining "knowing" and "doing." Here's the formula: knowing + doing = living. It's so much more powerful when they are ingrained. **Here are 5.5 simple steps to "live" the principles:**

1. Read — Read to understand. Many people read to "confirm." They (not you of course) read and think or say "I know that." Knowing is NOTHING. It's asking yourself "how good am I at that?" that leads to a real understanding of the principle. Reading to understand is a deeper and more powerful read.

2. Think! — Think about how each principle translates to your career and your life. Think about how you could be more successful if you mastered each principle. Think about what it will take for you to do that.

3. Rate Yourself — Assess your present skill level for each principle. Mark the page at the top with a number between one and ten.

4. Plan Yourself — Let's say you rated yourself a six at principle number ten, Prospecting for Probable Purchasers. What is your plan to raise your level of mastery to a nine at that principle? Make that plan, and put a deadline to start and a deadline to achieve.

5. Start Small, but START -- Select two principles that you almost have mastered. Figure out a way to improve on what you already have mastered. Then select two principles where you are not too good and figure out a game plan to get better at those. Most people are not good at what they don't enjoy. Your game plan to improve weakness should include how to have more fun in your weak areas.

"Fun" leads to improvement faster than "lessons."

5.5 Decide to dedicate to the self discipline to succeed. All of this information is useless to the individual who reads it and does not act. Decision to act and dedication to follow-through are the secrets. They don't sound like secrets. In fact they sound obvious. Therein lies the flaw and the opportunity. Most people are looking for the easy way. Those people will be looking forever. You have an opportunity to pass all of those people, and most of the rest. All you have to do is decide to do so, and dedicate yourself to doing it.

Most people will not do the hard work it takes to make success easy.

Don't be like most people.

Put your heart into your business

"You can not expect to be a success unless you believe whole heartedly in the value of your product. You interest people, first, by the thing you talk about; and, second, by the way you talk. Your talk will not ring true, your words will not carry conviction, unless you are thoroughly sold on the merit of you proposition. Believe in your goods. Be loyal to your Company. Put your heart in your work."

— *Excerpt from The Primer, 1923*

THE PATTERSON PRINCIPLES OF SELLING

1. ***Think!***

2. Self Belief ... The Most Convincing Characteristic of a Salesperson

3. Positive Mental Attitude is Determined by You, Not Others

4. Boot Camp Separates the Salesman from the Wanna Be Salesman

5. Survival is a Combination of Knowing and Doing

6. Studying ... the First Discipline of Knowledge

7. Your Library is the Artesian Well of Knowledge

8. Planning Prevents Wandering and Provides Direction

9. Use "Today Time Management"

10. Prospect for Probable Purchasers

11. Increase Business Connections to Increase Sales

12. Creating the Demand Converts Selling to Buying

13. A Prepared Demonstration Means Personalized!

14. Gain Interest with Information about the PP not the We-We

15. Questions Lead to Answers...Answers Lead to Sales

16. Listening Leads to Understanding

17. Less Sell-Talk Time Leads to More Buy-Time

18. Your Message Must Be as Compelling as Your Product to Engage the PP

19. An Objection is the Gateway to a Sale

20. Selling is Not Manipulating…Selling is Harmonizing

21. Complete the Sale with an Agreement to Buy…
Be Certain to Give Them a Receipt

22. Service is the Reputation for the Next Sale

23. Extra Service Leads to the "Testimonial Word"

24. Referrals are Better Earned than Asked For

25. Testimonials will Sell when the Salesman Can't

26. Advertising Brings Awareness…Testimonial
Advertising Brings Customers

27. If You Have Done Your Homework and Prepared
Well, It Will Be Evident in Your Sales Report Card

28. Competition Means Prepare to Be Your Best

29. Recognize and Thank Those Who Have Helped
You Succeed

30. To Get Loyalty, You Must GIVE Loyalty. The Four
Pillars of Loyalty are the Foundation for Building
Long Term Business and Personal Success.

31. Exercise Must Be Both Physical and Mental

32. Training is an Every Day Occurrence

33. Decide…It Doesn't Matter if it's Right or Wrong…
Decide

34. You Become Known by the Actions You Take…
Take Ethical Actions

34.5 *If it has been working for 100 years or more, don't
even think about changing it. Tradition is a sacred,
powerful, insurance.*

JEFFREY GITOMER

CHIEF EXECUTIVE SALESMAN

AUTHOR
Jeffrey Gitomer is the author of *The Sales Bible*, now in it's 18th printing. And *Customer Satisfaction is Worthless - Customer Loyalty is Priceless*, now in its 9th printing. Jeffrey's books have sold more than 350,000 copies worldwide.

OVER 100 PRESENTATIONS A YEAR
Jeffrey gives seminars, runs annual sales meetings, and conducts training programs on selling and customer service. He has presented an average of 115 seminars a year for the past ten years.

BIG CORPORATE CUSTOMERS
Jeffrey's customers include NCR, Coca-Cola, Cingular Wireless, Hilton, Sunbelt Rentals, Ty, Inc., Enterprise Rent-A-Car, Cintas, Milliken, Financial Times, Turner Broadcasting, Comcast Cable, Time Warner Cable, HBO, Wells Fargo Bank, Mercedes Benz, Baptist Health Care, Blue Cross Blue Shield, Hyatt Hotels, Northern Trust Bank, Wausau Insurance, Northwestern Mutual, Sports Authority, Glaxo Wellcome, Ingram Micro, XEROX, A.C. Neilson, Fuji Photo, IBM, AT&T, and hundreds of others.

IN FRONT OF MILLIONS OF READERS EVERY WEEK
His syndicated column *Sales Moves* appears in more than 85 business newspapers, and is read by more than 3,500,000 people weekly.

AND EVERY MONTH
Jeffrey's column appears in more than 25 trade publications and newsletters. Jeffrey has also been a contributor and featured expert in *Entrepreneur* and *Selling Power* magazines and *The Wall Street Journal*.

ON THE INTERNET

His two WOW websites — www.gitomer.com and www.trainone.com — get more than a thousand hits a day from readers and seminar attendees. His state of the art web-presence and e-commerce ability has set the standard among peers, and has won huge praise and acceptance from customers.

UP YOUR SALES WEB-BASED SALES TRAINING

A weekly streaming video (low cost – high value) sales training lesson is now available on www.trainone.com. The content is pure Jeffrey – fun, pragmatic, real world, and immediately implementable. This innovation is leading the way in the field of e-learning.

SALES CAFFEINE

A weekly "e-zine" sales wake-up call delivered every Tuesday afternoon to more than 75,000 subscribers free of charge. This allows us to communicate valuable sales information, strategies, and answers to sales professionals on a timely basis.

AWARD FOR PRESENTATION EXCELLENCE

In 1997, Jeffrey was awarded the designation Certified Speaking Professional (CSP) by the National Speakers Association. The CSP has been given less than 500 times in the past 25 years.

If you make a sale, you can earn a commission.
If you make a friend, you can earn a fortune.

— *Jeffrey Gitomer*

BuyGitomer, Inc. • 310 Arlington Avenue Loft 329 • Charlotte, NC 28203

www.gitomer.com • www.trainone.com • 704/333-1112 • salesman@gitomer.com

ACKNOWLEDGEMENTS AND THANKS

To the research and editing team of: **Amanda Desrochers**, **Rachel Russotto**, and **Laura Miller**: ... Thank you for sharing in my excitement for this book, and for your insight, research, and your weekends. This project would not have been possible without your constant hard work and nagging.

To **Adam Sakoonserksadee** for the powerful and provoking cover designs. Award winning design is rare. And appreciated.

To **Greg Russell** for an 11 year friendship and a heroic and masterful job of typesetting this manuscript. It embraces the content and makes the words jump off the pages into your eyes.

To **Mitchell Kearney**, a world-class photographer, for capturing my image in spite of my hair.

To the **NCR Senior Management Team** ... Thank you for being my customer and for supporting this project. And thank you for standing on tradition and continuing to believe in and implement John Patterson's Principles.

To **Barb Swinger**, of NCR: Thank you for your professionalism, your patience, your input, and your corporate insight. You are not only a pro, you are cool.

To the **Montgomery County Historical Society**: ... Thank you for access to your extensive archives, and thank you for your cooperation.

Research material used to find and corroborate facts and philosophies:
Selling Suggestions: Book Two Efficiency in the Business, Frank Farrington, 1913
The Sales Strategy of John H. Patterson, Roy W. Johnson and Russell W. Lynch, 1932
John H. Patterson Pioneer in Industrial Welfare, Samuel Crowther, 1926
Builders in New Fields, Charlotte Reeve Conover, 1939
He Who Thinks He Can, Orison Swett Marden, 1908
NCR News, Various Editions 1922-1927
The Primer, Various Editions 1887-1923

Photos courtesy of **Montgomery County Historical Society**, Dayton, OH